EARWITNESS

EARWITNESS

A Search for Sonic Understanding in Stories

Ed Garland

New Welsh Rarebyte is the book imprint of New Welsh Review Ltd,
PO Box 170, Aberystwyth, Wales, SY23 1WZ,
www.newwelshreview.com, @newwelshreview,
Facebook.com/newelshreview
Copyright © Ed Garland, 2019
ISBN: 978-1-9993527-6-9

Editor: Gwen Davies
Design & typesetting: Ingleby Davies Design
Cover image: By your/Shutterstock.com
Printed in the EU by pulsioprint.com

The publisher acknowledges the financial support of the
Welsh Books Council

Dedication

To Helena

Contents

Introduction   1

They Can Be Heard   6

Not Listening, Not Reading   22

Heart Songs and Audiographs   37

Seagulls Throughout   49

Not One Acute Sense   61

Some Filters   77

One Sound in Particular   93

Bibliography   97

Introduction

The essays in this collection examine the sounds contained within stories and novels. I think that unless the sounds in our favourite books are especially unusual, dramatic, or spooky, they escape our attention: everyone's eyebrows go up when I tell them that written sounds are what I write about. Their surprise and interest soon turns to enthusiasm – now they have another reason to read. Fictional sounds can offer us new ways to hear our surroundings, and each other, and ourselves, which is useful for me because hearing loss and tinnitus took control of my ears several years ago. I've found that reading about sound improves my experience of the audible world.

We do not value fictional sounds as we value fictional sights, places, or people, even though sounds play an important part in the plausibility and beauty of all those elements. I spoke to a novelist recently who was mortified when they realised they'd *forgotten* to put sounds in one of their books.

But it's okay – the book won an award, and nobody writes to them to ask where all the sounds are. I sometimes wonder if the status of novelistic sound is so low because we usually do our reading in silence, which is a relatively new and weird innovation in the history of literature. According to Steven Roger Fischer, in his *A History of Reading,* reading was strictly an out-loud activity for the first few thousand years of its existence. Silent reading, however, quickly caught on and became the dominant mode in Europe in AD 384, after St Augustine of Hippo caught his teacher, St Ambrose, looking into a book but not speaking its words aloud. 'His heart searched into the sense,' wrote Augustine, 'but his voice and tongue were silent.' Augustine presumably promoted this quiet practice, and plenty of other people liked it as much as he did, so by the sixth century, St Isaac of Syria could ecstatically declare of his own reading habits: 'I practise silence, [and] when with prolonging of this silence the turmoil of memories is stilled…, ceaseless waves of joy are sent me by inner thoughts, beyond expectation suddenly arising to delight my heart.' Sudden delights, ceaseless waves of joy – St Isaac of Syria was absolutely off his face on silent books. Maybe silent readers were unintentionally inclined to devalue descriptions of sound because silence was the key to producing literary MDMA. In 2019, readers are encouraged to judge the plot, to search for a hook on page one by which they'll be dragged into a wave of dramatic tension that will not allow them to pause. It is very hard to make a decent plot out of sound.

What I look for in a book, it turns out, is sonic experience. In 2006, the researchers Jean-Francois Augoyard and Henry Torgue produced a book called *Sonic Experience: A Guide to Everyday Sounds*. This is an encyclopaedia of sonic effects, some familiar, like echo, and some peculiar, like envelopment, 'the feeling of being surrounded by a body of sound that has the capacity to create an autonomous whole.' In their introduction, Augoyard and Torgue describe how 'everyone listens in their own way'. In these essays, I want to describe how paying close attention to fictional sound changed my day-to-day listening habits. I have moderate hearing loss and permanent tinnitus, and I acquired those conditions by acting like music was the only thing worth listening to, at maximum volume for the longest possible time. For years I pursued ceaseless waves of joy, and envelopment, and ignored some psychological issues which eventually became unignorable. My appetite for music left no room for the appreciation of sound – sound was boring because it wasn't music. I was always reading, usually with music in the background, but like apparently most other people, I paid no attention to the sounds in the stories.

Elias Canetti's *Earwitness* was published in English in 1979. A bizarre book, it consists simply of a list of characters who are each given a few pages of description. The Earwitness appears amongst the Home-biter, the Moon-cousin, and the Woe-administrator. An atmosphere of disapproval colours all the descriptions. The Earwitness is sneaky but he has his uses:

> *All these modern gadgets are superfluous: his ear is better and more faithful than any gadget, nothing is erased, nothing is blocked, no matter how bad it is, lies, curses, four-letter words, all kinds of indecencies, invectives from remote languages, he accurately registers even things he does not understand and delivers them unaltered if people wish him to do so.*

The rest of my book consists of a few attempts to unblock my mind's ear, to register, with some accuracy, the kinds of sonic understanding located between reading and listening.

They Can Be Heard

The loudest picnic I ever attended was on a Wednesday in October, 2017. My wife and I walked up the steep hill south of Aberystwyth's Tan-y-Bwlch beach to sit and watch the sea below. A bulky wind roared off the water, up the hill, up our noses and down our throats. Its salted noise was so copious and persistent that it easily covered up the ringing sound I've been hearing constantly for the last few years. I wanted to store this wind-noise somehow, so that during future ear-troubles, if I could emit it from my open mouth, its audible texture might soothe me. I chewed squishy scotch eggs and wedges of pork pie. When Helena spoke, I watched her lips move, so I could be reasonably sure of what she said. Mostly she said things about food and small triumphs. Since our wedding and our move from Bristol to Aberystwyth we'd spent months and months looking at this hill without walking up it, and now we'd walked up it and sat on it and shoved delicious lumps in our gobs with the loud wind smacking our jackets. We'd found a new sound to sit within.

Back at home I took a book from the shelf, *Grits,* by Niall Griffiths, which is set in Aberystwyth, and which formed my first impressions, years ago, with its addictive linguistic rush, of this place where I now live. The town's buildings and streets seem charged with the dark tones of the local fiction. I wonder which of the people sitting on the pavements or lying on benches might have served as models for the people in *Grits*. When I hear a group of students bellowing inanely in a pub, I remember the loathing Griffiths' characters never fail to produce in response to this vocal nuisance. I remember the many times I've bellowed inanely myself, both in groups and solo. The reason I took that book from the shelf this time was to see what it might say about the sound of the hill Helena and I had just sat on. Was it as loud in *Grits* as it had been for us?

The narrative is punctuated with regular 'excerpts' from a 'guide to West Wales'. It's not the sort of guide that encourages people to visit the places it describes, being heavy on lyrical foreboding and light on cheap restaurants. The sonic qualities of the landscape surrounding Aberystwyth are given a mystical mention: 'They can be heard, sometimes, the mountains, they can be heard as they shift closer; a deep, low rumble from within the earth followed by a slow and persistent grinding.' Then comes the response of the mountains across the water, in Ireland: 'the after-midnight keening of the Wicklow range at a pitch too high for the human ear, the reuniting of a partnership once perfect, once powerful, now lost.' The two groups of mountains are joined in sound, but remain sonically separated, one high, one low, as they are geographically separated by the Irish Sea. There's no roaring wind, but there is the pleasant suggestion that mountains make sounds we don't hear, and that these sounds carry meanings between regions of an emotional landscape.

I added Griffiths' mountains to my literary sound map of Wales. Material for this map comes from trawling Wales' English-language fictions for new sounds to read. While I try to come to terms with my damaged ears, reading about sound has helped me to listen more deeply, because some authors' writing can bring out the subtleties of sonic experience. My sound map began with Lewis Jones' Rhondda valley in the south, the west coast of Cynan Jones, and Brenda Chamberlain's Ynys Enlli, or Bardsey Island at the tip of the Llŷn peninsula, just visible across the roaring sea from where my wife and I sat snacking.

Before we moved to Aberystwyth, we lived in Bristol, an altogether louder and angrier place. Here was where the ringing in my ears shifted from intermittent to constant. For a long time I refused to accept the change. The best I could do was to be irritated all day and night, as if the sound were some grit in the brain that might be washed out by seething. When I wanted relief, I'd try and find other things to be irritated by. Anything would do: a less-than-perfect cup of coffee; a sign saying 'Smile! You're on CCTV!'; a landlord attempting to be matey. I'd needle myself with those things and rant about them in my head. I can't recommend this counter-irritation as a coping strategy, but it'll certainly help if you need to get better at being enraged.

Alongside the endless ring of tinnitus, I had the problem of muffled ears. When Helena moved into my flat, I was frequently confronted with my inability to understand her speech. Her consonants tended to blur – an 's' was an 'f' and a 't' was a 'c' and a 'p' was a 'b' and so on – so I had to make do with vowel sounds and context. I could not believe my luck that this woman wanted to live with me, and at the same time

I was ashamed that I lacked the capacity to hear her. There seems to be a limit to how many times you can ask someone to repeat themselves before the relevant moment passes and the words that belonged to it expire.

In the book, *Sound: Stories of Hearing Lost and Found,* Bella Bathurst describes her own hearing loss alongside the stories of musicians and shipbuilders who've experienced similar damage to their ears. She writes about the acoustics of internal experience, and what it feels like to know that people are speaking to you but not be able to hear what they say. 'The edges of sound are still there but the sense in its centre has gone.' My hearing loss is moderate compared to Bathurst's, but I experienced this loss-of-centre very often, when failing to grasp what Helena was saying in the early days of our relationship. I learned to watch her lips when she spoke so I could catch the words by their visual edges. But whenever I failed to grasp something, I also tried to notice how much I enjoyed the *sound* of her voice. She spoke to me in kindness, softly, so unlike how I spoke to myself. Her vocal tone and rhythmic contours became a defining feature of our one-bed flat's acoustic space, and this space extended into my auditory imagination, so whatever frustration came from the hearing loss and tinnitus was partly balanced by a kind of emotional reverb.

She encouraged me to have my ears tested. The first audiologist said the results were 'pretty nasty' and urged me to consider hearing aids. The second one was less sure. Hearing aids can cost half a year's salary or more. They don't restore your hearing as it was. It's more like they give you an amplified sound-world to deal with. They can open up new channels of irritation as well as understanding. I thought it might be more rewarding, and certainly cheaper, to work on changing my emotional response to the physical injury. I could try to listen more calmly to whatever sounds make themselves available.

Bathurst suggests that benefits might arise from altering our attitude to sound: 'If, instead of thinking of it as just noise, we thought of it as pressure or saw it as curves in the shape of time and space, then perhaps it would be easier to grasp its potential.' I think fiction can show us how to do this, just like it can alert us to the dangers of totalitarianism or describe the pleasures of meaningful work. Most of the English-language fictions of Wales I've read have moments of enhanced listening in them, revelations of the ear in which sound is shown to exert emotional pressure. We don't just hear sequences of audible incidents that carry more or less relevant information. We exist within sound whether or not we choose to give it our attention. Fiction can enrich our relationship with our ears, and improve our hearing, by showing how sound is a dimension we inhabit.

In *Grits,* the acoustic environment of the mountainous countryside includes the noise of military planes making unbearable noise as they pass overhead on training exercises. One character, Malcolm, says the plane-sound is 'like a hacksaw' in his bones. Another, Sioned, says, 'they give me the darks, they do – loud, threatening – you can be out walking by a lake or something feeling perfectly happy with everything and then one of those twats roars over and ruins it all and that's it then – you're on a downer.' This is a stark example of sound as emotional pressure, and of excessive volume as physical violation. There's always the chance that whatever tranquillity the countryside provides will be shattered by the screams of technology, especially on a day with clear skies and beautiful views. Sioned continues, 'Oh, the pilots need their training they say – aye – but no one can tell me that it's not also a show of strength – a threat – like, see what we've got to destroy you with – we can blow you to fuckin bits if we want.' The bodies of *Grits*' characters become conduits for sound's political resonance, as their skeletons rattle into mountains of grief.

The writer Brandon LaBelle, in *Acoustic Territories*, explores the varieties of meaning that sound can produce: 'The trajectory of sound... is a story imparting a great deal of information fully charged with geographic, social, psychological and emotional energy.' It's quite a lot like a definition of fiction. In the books I read when I first moved to Wales, I was struck by the sounds that seem to carry the energies described by LaBelle. In Lewis Jones' *Cwmardy,* the Rhondda valleys resonate with political audibility. The story's protagonist, Len, lives close to the coal mine, its industrial soundscape strangely organic: 'the pit had a life of its own... it was never still or silent, but was always moving and moaning in response to the atmosphere and pressure.' Every morning the pit hoots, to summon the men to work. As a child, Len grows to hate these alarm calls whose sound spreads over the valley. When he grows up and begins to work alongside his dad in the pit, the sound of the hooters 'blasting' the air with their warning call at five am becomes the signal that he has to move his body out of bed, to join the men who walk to work in a 'never-ending silent flow'. In *Cwmardy's* fictional sounds, we can hear the loudness of authority and the silence of obedience. But there's also something more complex in the valley's sonic qualities, and in the way Len responds to sound with his body while he develops a political ear. At the funeral of Len's sister Jane, the people sing a song, and its effect is extraordinary:

> *Its plaintive melody, palpitating and mellowed*
> *with grief, rose above the housetops of the village,*
> *and crept slowly up the sides of the surrounding*
> *mountains, whence it drifted back, matured music,*
> *to cover the valley with a blanket of shivering*
> *sound. The echoes re-entered the throats where they*
> *had originated and were reborn, more resonant*
> *and rounded, to be thrown again with greater*
> *vigour and clarity into the air. Here they hung,*
> *harmonising with the slow-moving funeral feet.*

Within his realist novel, Jones inserts this episode of hallucinatory attention to sound's physicality. When the congregation's song spreads out to 'cover the valley,' it achieves the massive sonic proportions of the pit's hooter. The echoes from the valley then enter the people's bodies by their throats and are transformed, re-emerging with more energy and a fuller shape, accompanied by the sound of feet making contact with the ground. All the sonic force produces a life-changing moment for Len, as 'the voices soak their music into his flesh.' This physical absorption of the song's power prompts a moral shift, and Len's character-defining ambition emerges: the struggle to improve working and living conditions in Cwmardy: 'The hill became a symbol to him…. The pit became an ogre to him…. He conjured the hill and the pit as common enemies of the people working in connivance to destroy them.'

Unlike Griffiths' mountains, which still regularly tremble under the noise of military pilots taking advantage of sunny days, the acoustic territory of Lewis Jones' fiction is no longer available in real life. *Cwmardy* is set between 1890 and 1920, and was first published in 1937. It contains sounds we won't hear again outside of museums or archive recordings. The valuable thing about fiction from this era is that it preserves not just the sounds of a place's past, but the effect those sounds produced amongst the people who lived in that vanished environment. Reading about how other people navigated through sonic effects I'll never experience has led me to consider my acoustic privilege. The graphs of my hearing test results look like valleys of diminished sensitivity, but I can see that this is a consequence of a contemporary luxury problem, which I worked – in physically comfortable locations where the only occupational hazard was boredom – to afford. I never had to build ships or dodge bullets or bellow across cacophonous factory floors. Luxury grows from the same root as lust. You keep pursuing it when it's obviously not good for you. I earned quietly and spent loudly and the loudness did what the warnings said it would do.

In *The Dig,* Cynan Jones considers the sonic dimensions of grief and absence. The book's protagonist is a farmer. In one scene, he notes the 'isolated private intimacy' of the houses across the valley from his farm. It's raining, and he's sitting in a barn thinking about his wife, who recently died: 'The cat came up and sat with him, and for a while they sat like that, in the comfortable sound of the rain, and the closeness of the cat was almost too much.' The farmer is *in* the sound of the rain. He and the cat do not hear the sound or listen *to* it; the sound is *where* they are, during a moment of still-raw grief heightened by the man's recent considerations of isolation and intimacy. This link between sound and loss is made as explicit as it could possibly be, when, later on in the book, the man remembers hearing but not seeing the moment of his wife's death, when she was kicked in the head by a horse.

> *He heard the crack, had sensed it almost as*
> *something that shouldn't be in the panoply of sounds*
> *about the farm. It had been the speed of it. And then*
> *he had heard the horse run. There had been a split*
> *second as he registered the sounds, and then he had*
> *become this thing that just tried to get to her as fast*
> *as possible.*

The devastating resonance of this event contorts the farmer's relationship to his local soundscape.

When the farmer hears the 'slice of the spades digging the ground' in the graveyard, the day before his wife's funeral, this gravedigging echoes the dig at the centre of the book:

the capture of a badger so it can be sold to a group of men who force it to fight dogs. The man in charge of digging into the badger's sett locates the position of the badger by listening as his dogs hunt for it. 'You could hear the barks moving through the ground... alternately sharp and muffled until they seemed to regulate and come with a faraway percussive sound.' He then walks to where he thinks the dig should begin. 'He seemed to swirl in some eddy, then came to a halt, as if caught up on something.' Another man has a device that can detect the position of the animals underground, but this merely confirms that the first man was already correct. Skilled listening gives him a sinister efficiency. He immerses himself in the sonic flow until he feels the snag of arrival.

Across the water north-west of Cynan Jones' coastal hills is Bardsey Island, where the writer and artist Brenda Chamberlain lived for fifteen years. In her book, *Tide-race,* she gives a fictionalised account of her search for the peace and space that would feed her creative work. She's sensitive to emotional acoustics. After the foreword, she says 'Listen: I have found the home of my heart,' and a sonic thread begins. As she sailed towards the island, it summoned her with sound: 'Clear as glass in the blue and gold day the rock Leviathan lying to the westward sent out an unending cry.' But her heart was uneasy and her new home was full of strange noises that accompanied the small island community's ambivalent atmosphere of cooperation, isolation and suspicion. One phrase she writes of the sea could summarise the island's psychological conflicts: 'Our minds grew dazed by the thunder of the conflicting tides.'

Sea-sound is often suggested as a treatment for tinnitus. If you listen to waves breaking at a low volume, they might gently wash over the constant ringing and mask it, or at least smooth its edges so it's easier to accept. In *Tide-race,* the sea does not soothe and Chamberlain does not accept. The acoustic force of the waves motivates her melancholy search for calm. Occasionally the water is 'blank and peaceful', but more often it's doing something to bother the ears during bad weather. 'The roaring of the surf is monstrous. It booms.... There is no escape from the raving of wind and water.' 'The waves talk hurriedly and hugely of death by drowning.' 'The sea was hungry; the noise of it had hurt our ears for days.' There are sea-caverns into which 'at times of storm the surf would burst like gunfire.' Chamberlain noted that the island has to accept every wave that comes to it, and has been doing so for a very long time. 'How can we rationalise and set to numbers pulsations of water that have been world without end?' She might have considered how her ears had to accept countless waves of sound in the same way. There was much to accept, and sound was never far from her thoughts. She suffered the 'screams' of oystercatchers, terns, and black-backed gulls, while the 'bottle-shaped guillemots' made the sounds of 'love-making, scolding and gossip'. But it's the shearwaters who provide the eeriest upset. Their cries are too human. She calls them 'night-spirits' and, like the fighter planes in Niall Griffiths' hills, they can really ruin the day. 'Shearwater after shearwater cackled and laughed until there was left no memory of the day's festivity.'

The final sound in *Tide-race* comes from Chamberlain's imagining of what might audibly emanate from the ruins of the island's chapel. There rises, she writes, 'as if from living choristers, a plain-chant from perished throats. They fill the house with their singing, but they are more than voicers of canticles, for in their disembodied state is lostness and yearning as if they felt too keenly the cold austerity of outer regions of space.' Having first been called by an 'unending cry' to the island, she now imagines, over a decade later, an unending isolation made audible by disembodied throats. She has listened to herself and discovered that she is not in the happiest state of mind.

I think reading things like this, with attention to the many ways sound is entangled with conscious experience, can improve our hearing. Not because it enhances our physical sensitivity, but because it encourages a more subtle consideration of sound's multiple planes of significance.

Not Listening, Not Reading

In February 2013, I found the twenty-third employer of my long non-career. I'd been signing on for a few months and picking up odd shifts in bars and kitchens, but had nothing regular. Scrolling through the vacancies on one of Bristol Central Job Centre's extra-sweaty touch-screens, I printed off summaries of all the vacancies I could possibly fill: retail assistant (again), driver (again), youth hostel receptionist-café person-cleaner (again) and also the bewildering opportunity to try something semi-new – the county court needed an usher, and there didn't seem to be a reason not to apply. I met all the essential criteria: I was a person who could perform simple tasks and say 'yes'. Also, I had experience in the usher's most crucial physical move: gesturing with the hand towards a door or a chair. When I was seventeen, I was an usher in the now-closed Odeon on Oxford Road in Manchester. I tore people's tickets and pointed in the general direction of their seats. When necessary, I was supposed to get these people to be quiet so as not to ruin the magic of *What Women Want* or *Dude, Where's My Car?* I thought I was a big fan of films and cinemas in general, but by the end of my first twelve-hour shift I'd realised I was only a fan of a few very specific films, none of which came to the Odeon. This realisation – combined with a lifelong commitment to never interrupting anybody for any reason, especially not if they were throwing popcorn at Mel Gibson's giant face – meant that I would quite often leave the auditorium during my shift, to sit in the corridor and read a book. I couldn't persuade my supervisors that this was the right thing to do, even when the books were about films. After a zesty discussion with three managers about my peculiar work ethic ended in a reprimand for eating a hot dog, I quit. Now, at twenty-eight, after passing the interview, I was going to be a different sort of usher, in Bristol County Court. I was a bigger fan of justice than I ever was of films, and to be in the building where justice was concocted, to maybe even assist the concoction of justice by pointing people towards their seats and delivering files to desks, made me feel – briefly – as if I might have a purpose. Which was useful, at the time, because I'd misplaced the will to live.

When I accepted the job and began my training, I had a head full of very loud and persistent thoughts about self-destruction. I'd failed to heed the optimistic message of *Dude, Where's My Car?*, despite having had more opportunities to see it than the people who were in it. Plus, I was having difficulty hearing things. I'd been listening to loud music through cheap headphones since I was nine years old, and going to gigs since I was sixteen. So along with the internal clamour of thoughts and urges, I had a constant ringing in my ears, and an inability to decipher the speech of quiet people. And the number of quiet people seemed to be on the increase.

To my ears, the county court's soundscape was made up of grumbles. Incorporating mutters, moans, whinges, grunts, tuts, sobs, growls, sarcastic laughs, pummelled keyboards and stifled laments, the variety of grumbles was huge and the supply inexhaustible. By ten am every morning the open-plan office was a cloud of sonic dissatisfaction. In the corridors and rooms in the rest of the building were the workload-grumbles of the judges in their chambers, the obscene grumbles of the security guards at the public entrance, the supportive-and-divisive grumbles of union meetings, the formalised grumbles of the court hearings, and the time-related grumbles of the public in the waiting areas. The waiting areas of all five floors were open to each other, so a squabble by the lifts at the entrance could bounce off the floor tiles and spiral sixty feet up the central staircase, to be absorbed by the carpet outside court number nine, under the feet of a grey-faced family who've been arguing about inheritance for so many years that there's no longer anything left for them to inherit. I soaked up all this audible discontent, blended it with my own morose supply, and overdosed on grumbles seven days a week. I agreed with my fellow ushers that ushers were treated like administrative donkeys. I agreed with the judges that judicial workloads were impossibly demanding. I nodded along while defendants in small claims cases called their opponents greedy fuckers. I laughed when a judge called a defendant 'a shit'. There was a theme tune that travelled round the building: a document trolley with a wheel so squeaky it sounded like an avant-garde jazz trumpet solo. It left invisible wires of irritation in the air around the desks it had visited. We tutted and moaned about it but never went out and bought the oil that would've made it silent.

My decline in mental health amplified the distress produced by my hearing troubles. At twenty-eight, I'd been listening to loud music at top volume for two decades. When I was nine or ten, top volume on a Walkman was thrilling. It made the music so big that there was no room in the skull for anything else. When I borrowed a tape of Nirvana's 'In Utero' from the local library, I was fascinated by all the clangs and howls of feedback, and I turned them up to the point where they almost hurt to hear. A few years later, drum n bass arrived in my brother's bedroom. It was a strange excitement, like blissful panic, a torrent of compression that was at its best when played so loud it shook my skeleton. It became my habit to play music as loudly as possible for as long as possible. At some point in my twenties, I noticed that the top volume of an iPod was never quite loud enough. So I started to buy the second-cheapest earphones on sale in HMV, instead of the white ones that Apple threw in for free with their devices. The new earphones shut out the sounds of the environment more effectively, and formed a tighter seal in the ear canal, so I could push more sonic energy into my head. Sometimes I'd wonder about the ringing in my ears that would linger for a while after I removed the headphones, or would linger for two or three days after a night out, and I knew that this was a clear sign of hearing damage. I didn't listen to the quiet voice that told me to change my behaviour to prevent the damage getting worse.

My twenties were my decade of not listening to the quiet voice of reason that told me to persist, to be open to opportunities, and to be kind to myself. But there was a brawl of other voices saying things like 'don't bother', 'have another delicious beverage', and 'kill yourself'. Those were the ones that had my attention. I struggled not to obey them, and when they got too troubling I used music to cover up their noise.

I never kept a job for longer than a year. The ringing in my ears came to stay forever, and I practised smiling and nodding at people when I didn't know what they'd said, and laughing when I hadn't heard the joke. By the time I got the court usher job, the music still hadn't worked as a way to silence my thoughts, but I had a complementary and equally useless strategy. I was that person of dubious virtue: a 'voracious reader'.

In *The Novel Cure,* Ella Berthoud and Susan Elderkin explain how books can work like medicine for mental conditions. 'Sometimes it's the story that charms; sometimes it's the rhythm of the prose that works on the psyche, stilling or stimulating. Sometimes it's an idea or an attitude suggested by a character in a similar quandary or jam [to the one you're in].' Reading Ali Smith's *There but for the* can cure a fear of dinner parties. Marilynne Robinson's *Home* is the antidote to turmoil. Supposedly, Jonathan Franzen's *Freedom* is the cure for tinnitus. *Freedom* is a 'wall of sound,' they say, with 'no brick missing, not a crack in the cement,' because it depicts every aspect of contemporary American society, and one of the characters has ringing in his ears. This ought to have been the novel that soothed my hearing and calmed my head, but when I read it, I didn't pay any attention to its events. What I liked about *Freedom* was that I found it in a charity shop and paid three quid for five hundred pages of words. Like turning up the music in my headphones, my method of bibliotherapy was to focus on the rhythm and tone of the words so much that I barely registered the story. I didn't care about motivations, conflicts or obstacles. I didn't bother analysing the characters' attitudes or measuring the hilarity of the pop-cultural references or considering what the book might suggest about socio-economic predicaments. I would just blast the words through my head at high speed and top volume. There was no time to admire the scenery or revisit any bits I didn't understand. I wanted words to fill my head so that my head might stop filling itself with troubling phrases. It was like trying to drown out an endless episode of *Question Time* by mumbling my way through the TV guide. *The Novel Cure* talks about 'the temporary relief of your symptoms due to the power of literature to distract and transport.' I had the distraction of the words, but because I didn't listen to what the words were saying, I never experienced the transportation of the stories.

I would read on my bed, sitting against the wall with my legs crossed. After a few minutes I'd find myself rocking back and forth in time with my heartbeat. Gradually, over the months, a grey stain bloomed on the wall where my greasy hair would smoosh against the off-white paint. I must have read a hundred books between February – when I got the job in the court – and the following December, when things finally collapsed and I was signed off work with a knackered head. I remember the titles of about ten of these hundred books. The ones I remember most easily are those that had characters who struggled to recognise whether their 'I' was their self or someone else's or no self at all and they just babbled in the dark until the book ended. Mostly that's Samuel Beckett: *Texts for Nothing, How It Is,* and *The Unnameable.* I'm not sure if I'd call those books novels, and I don't think they cured anything within me, but their self-lacerating confusion at least produced a resonance of familiarity in my head. *How It Is* was particularly user-friendly, since it has no punctuation other than gaps between blocks of text. It was unstoppable.

The focus on the rhythm and volume of the words rather than the events they represented is why I can only talk about my favourite writers in sonic terms. They all have beautiful tone. These tones are most beautiful when they're as loud as you can make them. Beckett's laconic percussion starts to cover up, or at least provide an interesting accompaniment to, the ever-ongoing emotional cacophony. It can be a great comfort to turbo-encounter sentences like 'That's right, wordshit, bury me, avalanche, and let there be no more talk of any creature, nor of a world to leave, nor of a world to reach, in order to have done, with worlds, with creatures, with words,' when your own head is expressing, for months on end, in an infinitely less fluent and more abrasive monologue, the desire to leave the world. You are a little bit less alone knowing Beckett has had your thoughts before. The most handy of his murky comforts is the famous final line in *The Unnameable:* 'I can't go on, I'll go on.' It seems absurd, now, to say I used this phrase as medicine, but I did. I broadcast it into my skull during tens of thousands of excruciatingly low moments. Then there came a time when it was no longer effective.

In December 2013, on a Tuesday at nine am, I walked out of the office. There was a clamour in my head between competing urges to kill myself by one method or another. It was as if someone had decided *for me* that I couldn't go on, and there was suddenly an enormous variety of ways I could put an end to things and all I had to do was choose one. There was a fall from a tall building or a leap in front of a train or the submersion underwater that attracted tantalising rumours of euphoria. I could not calm down, and I spent all my energy trying not to obey these urges. I walked over Bristol Bridge, across town, past the fountains and the harbourside, to the library. I had the idea that, out of all the books in the world, if I could get hold of Henry Miller's *Tropic of Capricorn,* its familiar clattering mess might slightly diminish the blather and whine of suicidal impulses. I found it on the shelf and took it to a nearby bench outside. I knew the first part of the ugly beginning: 'Once you have given up the ghost, everything follows with dead certainty,' and I knew it went on to mention something about a 'jangle and discord'. With my heart bouncing against my ribs, I anticipated the relief of reading these first lines.

When I opened the book, I found that I couldn't read. My eyes would take in two or three lines and then carry on moving off the page, go slack, not allow me to take in any more words. I tried it a few times, and it still didn't work. There was no more room in my head. I very slowly walked home.

Over the next few days, I tried to present a calm exterior for my housemates, tried to give the impression that, aside from perhaps needing a bit of medical help, I was doing alright, having an interesting time, although maybe sleeping a bit much and not showering as often as we'd all prefer. Occupational Health phoned, and urged me to start taking pills as soon as possible. When I saw the doctor, she urged me to try pills too, but she also pointed out that these pills frequently made people feel worse before they felt better. I thought that if I felt even one percent worse I wouldn't be alive. I would have rather carried on without a head, or lived in a shed on the moon, or been converted into a string of numbers and found a comfortable second life in an air-conditioned data storage unit where there'd be nothing to listen to except the soothing whirr of ones and zeroes. None of these things were available on the NHS, so the doctor found me some group CBT therapy. It was an hour's bus ride from my house. I went there twice before giving up, irritated by being asked to share things with a group of hyper-irritated people and two smiling facilitators who said 'thanks for sharing' every thirty seconds. But it at least made me realise, faintly, that a lot of people in Bristol had as much trouble listening as I did.

I went back to work in January. Everyone was very supportive. I discovered that I'd missed them. I still had a head full of doomy whines, but having responsibilities and colleagues gave me other things to try and focus on. The grumble-scape still dominated the air – exactly as it did before – but now I didn't find it as irritating. I started to train as a union rep, to support people by listening to their problems.

I found a therapist a half hour's walk from work, on the top floor of a tall house in a posh part of Bristol. The idea was that I would talk and she would listen and summarise, and through these summaries we might reach an understanding of what was going on in my mind. The therapist and I sat facing each other in identical Ikea tub chairs while I punctuated the silence with tuts and sighs and the feeling that I was buffoonish and bad at speech. Whenever I made an attempt to describe what had happened, my throat clenched up and I'd stare at the floor for five or fifteen minutes. But as the weeks went on, the silences shortened and the talking lengthened. We came up with a working model of what was troubling me, and how I could offset these troubles by paying more attention to the quiet parts of myself. A few months later, I talked so much during one session that I laughed when a phrase ran through my mind: 'I'm sick of the sound of my own voice.' All the talking had put an acoustic distance between myself and my cacophonous thoughts. After a while, I could read properly again.

One thing I've learned since this period is the most basic thing about literature: novels contain representations of people and events. It can be hugely rewarding to connect emotionally with these people and experience some of what they experience. Their consciousness can become a part of your own. But it's not possible to connect with them if all you do is hoover up words, enjoying the texture without discerning the shape. Ursula K Le Guin once wrote that 'reading is a means of listening', and that listening is 'an act of community, which takes space, time, and silence.' Voracious reading, in the frantic and noisy way I practised it, was not really reading at all. I didn't listen to what mattered, didn't provide any time and space in which characters could form and events could resonate. I remained voracious because my methods didn't satisfy the basic human appetite for stories.

Recently I had a look at our shelves to see if I recognised any books from my ushering period. Most of them must have gone back to the library. Franzen has gone to the Salvation Army. One book I could say I definitely read during that time was a great self-published novel, *The End of March,* by Lydia Unsworth. I remembered its unsettling clarity and its short blocks of text. I opened it to see what it might say about listening and sound. Straight away, on page one, there's a man called Sergei having a profound auditory experience. 'It was three months ago that a papery sound came into Sergei's life. A papery falling-through-stale-air sound. A papery metallic pushing-through sound. A disorientatingly demanding papery sound.' Later on, 'Sergei is thirty-two years old or thereabouts and he is lying on the ground-down tarmac of a nameless city listening to a river flow beneath and perpendicular to his horizontal feet.' Then he is 'trying to make the river louder' and 'losing this internal battle'.

Sergei's strange listening habits evoke the mental difficulties attached to unwanted sounds and inadequate hearing. While I'd failed to it notice at the time, I'd been doing exactly what's described in *The End of March*: trying to make quiet things louder, instead of loud things quieter. It hadn't worked. I'd lost the internal battle, and the loud urges, the competing commands, had nearly killed me. What I needed was Le Guin's blend of space, time, and silence, so stories and characters could grow in the mind's acoustic territory.

Heart Songs and Audiographs

I used to think Annie Proulx's 'Heart Songs' was a story about music, a nice wistful prose-album whose only purpose was to deliver its unrecorded songs into my head. Played in a kitchen somewhere in the 'brushy, tangled land' of rural north-east America by a family called the Twilights, these fictional songs thrilled me with what I imagined was their authenticity. The songs exist because the story's protagonist, Snipe, after moving to this brushy land in search of musical adventures, answers a 'musician wanted' advert placed by the Twilights in the local paper. He drives to their house and walks up to the porch, where 'a wood thrush hurled cold glissandos into the stillness'. The house's doorstep is a 'broken millstone', and 'threads of corn silk lay on the granite'. Inside the house, 'the stamped tin ceiling was stained dark with smoke... Above it hung a fly-specked calendar showing a moose fighting off wolves under a full moon.' The eyes of the Twilights, sitting in a half-circle, 'gleamed with the last oily shafts of August sunlight'. The father, Eno Twilight, tells Snipe to sit 'off to the side' in the empty chair 'with chromium legs and a ripped plastic seat'. When the first song begins, there is a 'hard, sad' singing voice, a 'cloying' harmony from a fiddle and a 'nasal, droning undernote' from the accordion. Snipe thinks the music is 'curious, but not disagreeable'. More songs follow, and Eno, we are told, 'played with extraordinary virtuosity', while his sister Shirletta 'twitched her little mouth and rang her mandolin like a dinner bell'. The musical details are vague. The songs emerge from the tears and cracks in the materials of the Twilights' home. I thought I was hearing authenticity. In my auditory imagination I gave the songs a grainy, plaintive texture and added the crackle of vinyl over the top, so they sounded like the American folk and blues music recorded by John and Alan Lomax: people singing on their back porches or in cheap hotel rooms, transferred to the compilation CDs I owned from ancient sibilant vinyl discs whose ineradicable hiss and crackle was an essential part of the listening experience. Years later, I discovered the Lomax recordings were not nearly as authentic and noble as I'd thought. While imagining the songs of 'Heart Songs', I pictured porch steps and beer bottles and microphones powdered with yard-dust.

I was living in Leicester and working at Virgin Megastore. I'd finished a degree in Music Technology which entirely cured me of my ambition to be a recording engineer or record producer or person who operated mixing desks with precision and confidence. After I'd dragged my brains through the final year's swamp of binary maths and acoustic conundrums, I could calculate reverb times for cathedrals and the absorption coefficient of the average household wall. I could only think of sound in terms of numbers and computer-aided visualisations, and since those terms were exhausting I wanted an indefinite break. I was happy to take my 2:2 and never hear the words 'music technology' again.

Virgin's instore radio station repeated songs frequently enough to qualify as sonic torture under the Geneva Convention. Our tragedy as employees was that the Geneva Convention only applied to prisoners of war. We couldn't persuade the managers that our ears and hearts deserved as much protection from musical damage as was given to captured soldiers. Richard Branson aimed his radio at customers who never lingered instore for long enough to notice the intense repetition of the playlist. Standing hungover behind the till, hearing Arctic Monkeys' 'I Bet You Look Good on the Dancefloor' for the fifth time in three hours during the weeks-long onslaught meant to boost Christmas album sales, one of my mental defences was to conjure up a soothing 'Heart Songs' classic like 'Silver Hooves' or 'The Trout's Farewell'. These fictional songs were perfect because they were different every time and they did not require sound waves for their power. They tickled my heart without troubling my Megastore-addled earholes, and they emerged from the best of all analogue formats: printed text mixed with light and absorbed by the body.

Around this time I also worked the bar at an indie club called Mosh. This was the tail-end of lung-cancer's glory days, and to work there was to inhale industrial amounts of Marlboro Light-smoke whether you wanted to or not. People were thirsty, and if they didn't want something that came from a bar tap, to which they could point, I had to move an ear towards their tipsy mouth and have them scream their order loud enough to overcome the carcinogenic jangle of The Smiths. Earplugs were available, eventually, but when I put them in I couldn't hear what anyone was screaming. I'd give them San Miguel when they'd asked for 'same again', so I took the earplugs out and left my ears completely open to all the large and frantic sound waves, and knew that I was at risk of causing permanent auditory damage, but the too-few good songs sounded so thrilling that I didn't care.

Although I'd binned the idea of becoming a sound engineer so I had more time to pursue depression, I still tried to make my own music when I wasn't at the club or the pub or the Megastore. My musical ideas were a world away from the Twilights' banjos and mandolins. I wanted to make bass-heavy monsters that had the mood and weight of producers I loved, like Dillinja and Amon Tobin. To make this music, I used a program called Reason that simulated the basic components of a studio: samplers and sequencers, compressors and effects units. You could create an endless number of these devices, load them up with sounds and arrange them into absolutely almost-banging tunes. Time would vanish in the making of details, layering drum patterns and chopping up guitar loops and adding shades of distortion to basslines. And nothing ever sounded quite right. I would add more and more filter sweeps and intricate snare-rolls, but the tunes never turned out how I heard them in my head.

I might have thought about what happened to Snipe during his first visit to Eno's kitchen:

*Snipe was carried along by the sound, he played in
tune and on time, yet he rode on top of the music
like a boat on a wave because old Eno wouldn't
make room for him, would not let them open the
set pattern of their songs even a crack to let him
play a riff or break or move out a little from the
body of sound. Snipe, the outsider, was cast into a
background corner, a foreign tourist who did not
know the language, who would not stay, who was
only passing through.*

Snipe can't communicate: he lacks the sonic articulation necessary to become immersed in the musical flow. There is an obvious symmetry between his physical position on a chair 'off to the side' of the Twilights and his artistic position in a 'background corner' of the music. Snipe never finds the creative solution that would allow him to complement the music and 'join the body of sound.'

The music I made on my laptop always had the flaw of fullness. Always adding layers and details and textures and weights, I never left any room in the music – I would invite people to listen to it, and they would find there was no way in.

I gave up the habit of making music a couple of years after I left Leicester and moved to Bristol. It wasn't an explicit decision to give up – when I clicked the red 'X' in the top-right of the Reason window for the last time, I didn't know it would be the *last* time. Days and weeks went by and I realised I had no desire to resume this habit that used to be a nightly obsession. My tinnitus was not yet permanent, but my depression was going from strength to strength. I'd discovered all sorts of ways to be unkind to myself, and my head hosted a chorus of intrusive declarations, a constant stream of judgments focused on my ever-growing worthlessness and the deplorable deception I practised, on a daily basis, by covering up this worthlessness and appearing to be someone who liked to enjoy themselves. I still heard music in my head, but made no attempt to bring it out through a computer, and this lack of effort was another strand of the judgment-chorus that chanted away at me during waking hours. Working in the music industry and making music were what I was 'supposed' to be doing, said the chorus, but having given it up, I now had nothing to contribute to the world and therefore ought to stop wasting the world's resources and give up life itself. I knew this was the result of faulty reasoning, but it was the loudest result in my head, and it repeated itself with the tirelessness of propaganda.

I re-read 'Heart Songs' a couple of years ago because I wanted to hear the old tunes again. I couldn't remember their names, but I hadn't forgotten their sound. It turns out 'Heart Songs' is really about a dickhead musician who ruins everything with his selfishness. Unmysteriously, I had been unable to see this aspect of the story when I was a twenty-something musician myself.

At the start, as Snipe drives towards the Twilights' home for their first meeting, we hear 'gravel snapping against the underside' of his car. 'Snapping' is a sonic symbol, both percussion and rupture, the sound of things being pushed too far, and of materials giving way under strain. Snipe is motivated only partly by the wish to play music. The driving force of his character is a kind of nihilistic voyeurism. While living on the money his girlfriend, Catherine, receives from her parents, he finds a 'dirty excitement' in the visible evidence of the Twilights' poverty. 'What he liked was the failing kitchen chair, the wrecked pickup in the weeds.' Unable to play anything that complements the Twilights' songs, he is still delighted because 'these were real backwoods rednecks and he was playing with them. They were as down and dirty as you could get.' His search for musical authenticity, 'the real stuff' as he calls it, is only the pretext for his 'secret wish to step off into some abyss of bad taste and moral sloth.' Snipe creates this abyss in the same place the music is made: the Twilights' kitchen. On an unannounced visit to the house one afternoon, he has sex with Nell Twilight. He thinks Nell is Eno's daughter, but she's really his wife. This brief encounter takes place as Nell is making jam ('jelly') in the kitchen and the men of the family, Eno and Ruby, are working in the nearby woods. Ruby injures his hand, and the two of them come into the kitchen for first aid, where they meet Snipe, realise what's happened between him and Nell, and chase him away. The sounds of irreversible actions are threaded throughout this decisive moment. In quick succession we hear chainsaws 'as monotonous as the night cicadas', 'the thrashing fall of a tree', the tearing of paper, and 'the scorched jelly crackling in the kettle'. As Snipe drives away from this scene, having narrowly avoided a beating, he says 'Goddamn hillbillies' to his rear-view mirror. At home, he quickly convinces Catherine that it's time to leave town. He doesn't really like Catherine, but knows her parents will provide money for them both.

They lie on the couch together after making the decision to leave, and 'with the dry feeling that he was saying catechism,' Snipe 'rested his mouth against the beat' of Catherine's heart. They drive on, and the story ends as his hands beat a 'Tex-Mex rhythm against the wheel'.

The critic Phillipp Schweighauser's book, *The Noises of American Literature, 1890–1980,* is a study of how the fiction of Theodore Dreiser, Thomas Pynchon, Don DeLillo and others registered the sounds of twentieth-century America's social and industrial development. Within this massive project, Schweighauser coins a term for those sounds that associate themselves with a character: the audiograph. This handy word describes 'a set of distinctive acoustic properties' designed to position characters within their fictional worlds. The audiograph can include accents and other vocalisations as well as the sounds people bring to life when their bodies interact with their environments. In 'Heart Songs,' Snipe's audiograph is defined by those sounds of rupture that seem to follow him wherever he goes, and the percussion that powers his car. I missed these small details on my first readings of the story, as I missed the larger point that Snipe is not some humble guitarist, trying to find other musicians to play with in a small town far from home. His name itself is a bit of a clue – it does not suggest generosity or consideration. But I didn't often look for any connections between the smaller and the larger parts of the stories I read in my twenties. I just wanted authors to either take me somewhere nice, like Proulx, or to impress me with disturbing prose, like Burroughs. I certainly didn't think that any writer might want to tell me something about myself, or to make me listen to my own audiograph.

The sounds that adhered to my character, in those years in Leicester, would have included the tsst-clop of opened lager cans, the regular drunken heckle, and most of all, the infinite complexity of lung-noise. Most of my friends and I were dedicated to inhaling smouldering substances through tubes of paper or ceramic pipes, and while these substances filled our blood with toxic treats and our heads with shit ideas, they also filled our lungs with sound: knackered accordions, distant sirens, and crestfallen cats all played together in riffs of aerobic dissonance. Now that I've stopped inhaling so much burning waste, my lungs have repaired themselves. Why can't my ears do the same? Has anyone tried removing human lung-tissue and implanting it into the screaming ears of the hearing-damaged and tinnitus-afflicted? Is that constant ringing noise a kind of auditory wheeze?

I've managed to shed many sonic belongings, and now I think (and hope) my audiograph is less hectic. One of the key features of this new audiograph is the request for people to repeat themselves, because most people I meet seem to mumble. Nobody else can hear my tinnitus, so I don't think I can include it in my graph. In my ideal world, though, everybody's tinnitus would be audible. It wouldn't have to be so loud that we could hear someone with tinnitus approaching from a distance, or a group of us pinging and whining round a library table. I would give tinnitus the intimate audibility of a heartbeat, that requires the ear to be placed against the body, so our loved ones could hear us ring.

Seagulls Throughout

When I moved to Bristol, I discovered seagulls could meow. One, in particular, liked to meow and yelp and yowl outside my bedroom window whenever I was trying to sleep through a hangover. Even at a quiet volume, the gull's obnoxious yelling would seem to stab my inner ears and unbalance my mattress. To make things worse, the gull would pause, giving me the chance to try and rush back to sleep, but the vocals would always resume, and eventually I'd have to leave my room and find somewhere else to pray for water and snacks and death.

I didn't have permanent tinnitus then. I only knew it in its temporary form, as a standard feature of mornings after visits to loud nights at Lakota or the Black Swan. I'd wake up with a kind of bitter fur pulsing in my mouth and smoke-infused sweat congealed on my skin and a ringing in my ears. None of these things were alarming. They were the standard residues of decent nights, the bodily trophies of immersion in the pressure waves of music that had attracted me to the city since I first heard the weird textures of Bristolian drum'n'bass when I was fifteen. I'd record Fabio and Grooverider's 2am Radio 1 shows onto tape in my suburban Manchester bedroom and listen throughout the week, at maximum volume through cheap plastic headphones. The tunes from Bristol producers like DJ Die and Krust all had a strange edge that I found addictive. I got to hear more of it as a sixteen-year-old when we had a dial-up internet connection, and the Drum n Bass Arena would broadcast live from nights in London or Manchester. Long before a bouncer ever let me into a club, I lent my ears to nightlife through 56k RealPlayer connections. To say '56k' is to say the sound quality was pretty much the same as when people today accidentally phone you from their pocket while they're out having a nice time. But the quality didn't matter, because a better one wasn't available and because the experience of hearing the tunes playing fast, rippling through bodies and bouncing off walls, and MC GQ making everyone make noise, and all the calls for rewinds, and knowing that sometimes all this was happening a few miles up the road at that very moment, was a genuine rush. Most DJs would play something Bristolian. Even if I didn't know the specific tune, it would be obvious that it came from

Bristol's Full Cycle or Dope Dragon labels. Although every artist had their own identifiable approaches – for example, Krust would build a bassline in a way that Roni Size never would – all their music seemed to produce the same atmospheric conditions: a thick space, a weighty bounce, a reassuring roll. By the time I actually got to Bristol in my twenties, these musical conditions had evolved, producers were using brighter sounds to construct their tunes, and dubstep had opened up new routes to moody euphoria. After a night out seeing The Bug or Doc Scott or Remarc, I was glad to wake up with tinnitus because it meant I'd brought my life into line with my musical priorities. The lacerating gull-noise that came through the window, however, was an unexpected element of the city's soundscape.

I'd always thought the voice of a seagull was essentially pleasant. As Richard Smyth puts it in *A Sweet, Wild Note* 'the twanging *pyah pyah pyah* bawled from a fishing village chimney was – and still is – the sound of a summer holiday.' Smyth's holidays were on the Yorkshire coast, while mine were in Wales, but in both places and thousands of elsewheres, the gull's barbed alarm calls are a cheerful sensory garnish for sandcastles and sunlit chips. So the spiky, raspy meows I heard in my early-twenties' hangovers were a form of sonic disillusionment. The seagull's vocals lost their association with long-gone happy events, and began to provide the theme-shriek of urban hangovers. I carried on going out to loud places and finding a sense of safety in hazardous waves of sound pressure, and, at some unnoticed point, a ringing in the ears became a feature of every morning and afternoon and evening, no matter where I'd been the night before. I'd acquired my own personal seagull, with a very high voice and bottomless lungs, who lived in my head and who would not shut up.

The supreme novel of seagull-sound is also one of the classics of Welsh writing in English: Bernice Rubens' *I Sent a Letter to my Love*. This novel of disquieting charm tells the story of a brother and sister who live together into middle age. The action centres on Amy Evans, for whom the seagull's cry is 'the sound she liked most'. Amy renders this sound as '*cawl*,' a word which is also the second syllable of her hometown, Porthcawl. Whenever she hears the seagulls, she hears a comforting echo of the name of the place in which she's lived all her life. She also likes to emit this sound herself. Throughout her childhood, she says '*cawl*' out loud as a kind of 'talisman' to make herself feel better during low moments. She has many opportunities to practise making herself feel better since she's so often slapped by her mother. One day she dodges her mother's raised hand and runs to the beach, crying '*cawl*, *cawl*' and hoping to hear the gulls join in. When none turn up, she hears her own voice 'crying alone', and this event represents the loss of 'the heart of her childhood'. She really, really likes to hear a seagull – the sound is at the centre of her life.

By the time Amy reaches middle age she's lost all her teeth from eating sticks of rock with 'Porthcawl' written all the way through them. Her technique for eating them is to cover the left half of the stick with her thumb and nibble down on the right, 'so that only '*cawl*' was visible.' So even when she couldn't hear her favourite sound, she could still eat it. And she ate it until it destroyed her teeth, and by the time she's fifty she lives 'abrasively side by side' with her brother, Stan, in what was their childhood home. Amy is a full-time carer for Stan, who has to use a wheelchair because of his rickets. The events in Stan and Amy's life are as repetitive as the seagulls' calls. Every morning, their friend Gwyneth comes round for breakfast, and the three of them have the same conversation and disapprove of the same things. Anything vaguely sexual is dismissed as 'disgusting'. When Amy finally tires of this routine, it's because she hears 'the hollow of the old performance'. She'd rather be hearing a seagull say '*cawl*', or saying it herself. I don't want to spoil the plot by revealing what Amy ends up doing to break the monotony, but I will mention she has the habit of uttering 'fuck, fuck' in public at people she doesn't like. It's a kind of thrilling transgression that keeps people away, a sonic weapon, a seagullism. While 'fuck' isn't as accurate a rendering of seagull-sound as '*cawl*,' it's still accurate in terms of attitude. It's not hard to imagine that seagulls are experts in incoherent cursing. Amy's life story is partly the story of how she valorises, imitates, dwells in and consumes this strange bird-sound.

After finishing *I Sent a Letter to My Love,* the loathing for seagull-sound I'd developed during Bristolian hangovers had softened into an intrigue: I thought I might use fiction to rehabilitate the gull-cry and make it into as much of a comfort for me as it is for Amy Evans. I looked for seagulls in every book I picked up. In the short story anthology *Urban Welsh,* Thomas Fourgs hears the gulls 'flying, to perch on chimney pots, atop orange mushroom-like houses and laugh, as if pinching someone's nose over and over.' In the same book, Niall Griffiths' story features a gull at a crucial moment, and 'in the mourning of its call is all thwarted reaching, all disappointment on the earth.' The fictional urban gull is a crooked, gloomy creature.

My copy of *Ulysses* tells me it's the 'most significant novel of the twentieth century'. Its seagulls are entirely silent. Our hero, Bloom, buys the gulls a Banbury cake as he walks across Dublin's O'Connell bridge. 'Those poor birds,' he thinks, tearing the cake into pieces and throwing it over the side, where the gulls swoop in to eat every crumb and make no sound at all. 'Lot of thanks I get,' thinks Bloom. 'Not even a caw.' Does this mean that the seagull's call is not a 'fuck, fuck,' but a 'thanks, thanks'? Do they sit atop their chimneys and scream their gratitude into the sky?

I was in Ystwyth Books in Aberystwyth, sniffing the air and dragging my ears across dusty spines, when I came across Alan Sillitoe's *The German Numbers Woman*. Page one, seagulls, 'fractiously squealing'. Perhaps these gulls, being positioned on page one, would be a feature throughout the book. I took it downstairs to the till and handed over three quid and looked forward to discovering whether these gulls' fractiousness would find a harmonious resolution.

There are some books and authors I have the feeling I'm 'supposed' to read. They're very hard to read, these authors, because the status they've accumulated over the years makes a clanging noise in my mind that obscures the faint whistle of my own judgement. It's nearly impossible simply to read the words on the page of a book I'm 'supposed' to read without wondering whether the feeling that has emerged in response to the words is the feeling I'm supposed to have. If I do like it, is that because I'm being pretentious? If I don't like it, is that because I'm not paying enough attention? It can take a couple of years of false starts – of trying the first few pages and putting it back on the shelf – before a book that's supposed to be brilliant begins to seem like it might be worth reading. Some of them are really worth the effort, like *Moby Dick* and *Ulysses* and Edith Grossman's translation of *Don Quixote*. All three of these are bizarre and funny and challenging. Alan Sillitoe is one of those authors I felt I was 'supposed' to read. I had the vague idea he was good at realism, that his stories were vivid and authentic. Maybe some of them are, but *The German Numbers Woman* is the worst book I have ever read in my life.

Admittedly, I read it with a head full of seagulls, which wouldn't help anybody reach a decent judgment.

The German Numbers Woman tells the story of Howard, a retired radio operator who was blinded in the war when his plane was attacked. He spends his retirement playing with his radio equipment. The German numbers woman herself is the voice of a strange coded broadcast, slightly mysterious but not essential to the plot. Very slowly, while Howard listens to this woman and other people exchanging Morse code and chatter from ships and planes and weather stations, he is drawn into a drug-smuggling caper that involves him having to sail from the UK to the Caribbean and back, on a boat full of career criminals, listening out on the radio to check that the police haven't detected their journey. Howard is eager to sail, because it gives him the chance to meet Judy, who he's overheard (while scanning the drug-smuggling airwaves from his house) expressing a passionate longing for Carla, her lover. At one point, the gulls, 'aeroplaning above the chimney pots', tell him that he ought to talk to his wife, Laura, about his plans. My tinnitus whined. My ears folded in on themselves. When the smugglers' boat lands in the Caribbean, Judy's boarding scene reads like the first draft of a piss-take. She drops a bag of pineapples and says 'let some prick take these to the galley. I'm shagged out and pissed off, and I want to get my head down.' The crime-boss kicks the bag of pineapples and one of them rolls up against Howard's foot. He picks it up and sniffs it. End of scene. It's entertaining for sure, but there's no hint of irony. Naturally, adventurous twenty-eight-year-old Judy is keen to have passionate sex with retired radio operator Howard as soon as possible. When it happens, Howard understandably employs 'an expert touch lulling her into an ease that made her lose all sense of where she was.' Then she says, 'Let's go to my bunk. I want all of you now.' Later on, I'm sorry to report, she says to Howard 'I want you in me all the time.'

As a baffling complement to this stomach-churning romance, Sillitoe keeps us relentlessly informed regarding what food and drink there is on the boat. The cook's name is Ted Killisick, a surname that expertly joins the rhythm of 'Sillitoe' to the idea of vomiting to death. Nearly every time Killisick's in a scene, someone's telling him how good a cook he is. It starts on page 269, where there's 'the smell of a savoury meal from Ted Killisick's galley'. Five pages later, 'I'll sit you down to a Killisick fry-up.' 280: 'Eggs, sausages, tomatoes and fried bread... Killisick's good at that sort of thing.' Three pages later: 'Ted promised hamburger steaks with all the trimmings... he's a dab hand as a cook.' At the bottom of this *same page* someone wants to know if there's enough drink on board. Well of fucking course there is, but how much? 'Enough to take us to Doomsday City and three times back. Just ask Ted Killisick, if you feel the need.' Page 306: 'Ted Killisick in the galley provided nonstop food and drink'. 313: 'I wonder what Ted's got cooking in the galley?' 334: 'Can't fault the food, Mr Killisick.' And, by the end, when the smugglers have been discovered because Howard has deliberately informed the police of their journey, Ted has his final say: 'I was hired as a cook, that's all I know.'

By this point my bad mood had evaporated and I'd abandoned the search for seagull-sounds and was simply enjoying myself. I was so glad Sillitoe kept producing clanging phrases and bizarre writing tics. If his novel was any 'better', if he had tidied up the text so that it met the middlebrow conventions of efficiency and transparency that are supposed to equal 'good prose', the book would have become just another mediocrity.

The snags in the text are the only reason it's worth looking at.

I was working as a court clerk once and, for various boring reasons, a witness giving evidence under oath claimed that they'd hated 'all three' of the *Fifty Shades of Grey* books. Nobody asked them why, if they didn't like the first one, they felt they had to read the other two. The only possible reason I can think of to read a trilogy you don't enjoy all the way through would be 'to check if the seagulls on page one were going to become a feature of the trilogy's fictional world, and, if so, would their audibility bear any significance, your honour.' In my case, the seagulls in *The German Numbers Woman* do have a dramatic function. They call to Howard that 'he must talk to' his wife Laura about his crime-plans. They tell him he lives 'in an indifferent universe', they howl and cry 'about their hardships'. Unlike Amy Evans, Howard develops no attachment to their sound. They seem to provide an acoustic mirror for his worries. My relationship with seagull sounds is no different after my trawl through their literary representations. Their sounds are still difficult to accept. There's an emotional issue here I don't want to examine, some sonic residue from life in Bristol that I haven't yet shifted, something that makes me more of a Howard than it does an Amy Evans.

Not One Acute Sense

In the spring of 2018, my tinnitus split in two. On the left hand side, I still have the familiar constant ringing sound, but on the right-hand there's now a rapid fluttering that comes and goes, a bit like a drunken Skylark practising a one-note improvisation. I prefer to encounter drunken Skylarks outdoors, along with Chaffinches and Willow Warblers and other birds who have interesting things to say. Given the choice, I wouldn't invite anything with a beak to come and talk inside my head forever, but apparently that's what I've done.

This change in composition was a setback. While I'd accepted that the tinnitus would be a part of my life, I hadn't anticipated that it might develop its sound, that it might expand its presence in my interior auditory space, so that instead of seeming to live in the centre of my head, it now had two poles, between which my consciousness was strung. I'd taken for granted that the sound would continue to do the same thing it had always done. The new, stereo, style took up more of my attention, and I felt absurdly betrayed, as if my ears had broken the terms of a contract. When I began to accept the tinnitus, before it went stereo, I failed to specify that I was accepting it as it was and only as it was. Its metamorphosis was a reminder that I had less control of my interior world than I wanted. I had to acknowledge that I'd been a little bit smug about how I'd accommodated this sound. I worried, too, that it might divide itself again, and I'd then have four ringing things to listen to instead of two, and might it not also carry on dividing itself in the same way, until my head was suspended in a proliferating geometry of pings and chatters and whines?

I needed to squash my worries. I started to read *Tinnitus: Clinical and Research Perspectives,* by the audiologists David M Baguley and Marc Fagelson. In their introduction, they discuss some examples of tinnitus in fiction. Thomas Hardy's *A Pair of Blue Eyes* features a man called William Worm, who describes a constant noise that only he can hear: 'Tis for all the world like frying fish: fry, fry, fry, all day long in my poor head, till I don't know whe'r I'm here or yonder.' I like how specific this man is about his tinnitus: it sounds precisely like *fish*, rather than any of the other things people might have fried in 1873. He's a good listener, and I was excited to think Hardy might have given William Worm's troubled but discerning ears a central role in his novel. But no: 'this high-frequency tinnitus plays no further part in the plot.' The next book the audiologists mention is Martin Amis' *Money*. In *Money*, a man called John Self describes a form of tinnitus that sounds like many different things: 'Jet take-offs, breaking glass. Ice scratched from the tray,' and 'computer fugues, Japanese jam sessions, digeridoos.' This isn't tinnitus 'as generally experienced,' say the audiologists, but more of a 'formless auditory hallucination'. It gets worse in a context of stress, though, which *is* a key feature of the general tinnitus experience, as well as of the reading-Martin-Amis experience, which is why I can't say anything more about *Money*. Baguley and Fagelson then suggest that tinnitus occurs rarely in fiction because it's generally considered a banal experience, 'like cleaning the bathroom' or having a headache. I'm not sure about this. I think novelists tend to throw banal things into their stories to add a bit of realism. There's also a distinction between the temporary and the permanent. If you had a headache that hadn't gone away after three and a half years, it would have become a central feature of your experience. William Worm's tinnitus is with him 'all day long'. He would have benefited from some bibliotherapy, which is one of the treatments suggested by Magdalena Sereda and Derek J Hoare in their chapter of *Tinnitus: Clinical and Research Perspectives*. Bibliotherapy involves reading about tinnitus to increase your understanding, and decrease misunderstandings, or 'negative false beliefs', about what has happened and is happening to your ears. Having better information on the condition can reduce distress, and allow people to make informed decisions about how to manage their auditory health. Informative reading is an essential part of self-care for people with tinnitus and hearing loss, but I would argue that wherever the idea of reading-for-health is presented – whether in leaflets, research papers, or online – its scope is always limited. We ought to be encouraging people with tinnitus and hearing loss to read *beyond* their conditions, to learn about sound in general rather than sound as an auditory problem. Descriptions of sounds and acts of listening, whether they're in novels, poems, nature writing, philosophy or anywhere else, can remind us that our damaged ears can still enable us to have subtle and fascinating auditory experiences.

Reading Margiad Evans helped me to enjoy listening to the world again, after my tinnitus changed its habits in 2018. Evans is probably best-known for her novels, like *Country Dance* and *Turf or Stone,* that describe violently complex relationships set within small towns and countryside dwellings. It's in her later works, though, where Evans makes her most detailed observations of sonic experience amongst her intense descriptions of plants and land and accounts of her health, which was declining because of a brain tumour that was starting to give her epileptic seizures. When she wrote, in *Ray of Darkness,* 'I have not one acute sense unless it be my hearing,' she was being hard on herself: her mind's eye was as sharp as her mind's ear. But her persistent examinations of the sounds she encounters does set her apart from her contemporaries, and makes her more like Henry David Thoreau and Richard Jefferies, writers she loved and whose subject was nature. In *Autobiography,* Evans is always working, whether it's in her garden or her house or on one of the local farms, as well as on the fiction and poetry she produced throughout this period. Most days, it seems, she still made time to sit and listen. Here she is having a lie down in a field:

I heard a lark's song, like a nucleus, very high and
rarefied, swarming in the sky; and minute sounds
broke off the hills – a lamb's bleat, the grunt of
a wagon wheel rolling over stones miles away.
Putting my face down I could hear an undertone of
distance, distinct and dwindled... the wheat hissing
round the edges of the fields, the sweet roar of
pollen-seeking bees in the willows, even the minute
crinkling noise the insects made creeping over
grass blades.

This episode records not just the sounds themselves but their interrelationships, and how they seem to be situated or embedded in the landscape, waiting to 'break off' from the whole, like audible crumbs. I like how she puts her face down in the grass to hear the 'crinkling' of walking insects, reminding us that we listen with our bodies, that we're in contact with the ground and supported by the earth. While noting the tiniest sounds, Evans doesn't lose the sense of distance that comes from her audible connection to the unseen edges of nearby fields. The bees she hears make a 'sweet roar', which is somehow more dramatic and gentle than the usual buzz.

This kind of comprehensive sound-survey prefigures the acoustic conservation work of R Murray Schafer, who popularised the idea of the soundscape in the early 1970s, thirty or more years after Evans wrote *Autobiography*. In his book *The Tuning of the World,* Schafer suggested 'only a total appreciation of the acoustic environment can give us the resources for improving orchestration of the world soundscape.' He wanted to treat the world as 'a macrocosmic musical composition', and sometimes, crusading against noise pollution, he sounds more than slightly daft. 'The world soundscape has reached an apex of vulgarity in our time,' he writes, revealing that his 'total appreciation' of the acoustic environment did not include those sounds that don't fit in with his eco-musical ideology. I imagine, in the early days of soundscape theory, that a great deal of tutting could be heard whenever an unwelcome sound offended Schafer's ear. Although Evans did share Schafer's distaste for the engine-driven sounds of the industrial and the urban, she spent far more time being an appreciative listener than she did being an acoustic policewoman. This appreciative attitude is what makes her writing so useful to my auditory health. It moves my mind away from those sounds I wish I couldn't hear, and gives me new words with which I can recognise sonic details.

In the book *Sonic Possible Worlds,* the writer and artist Salomé Voegelin suggests the term 'textual phonography' as a way to describe the written record of an act of listening. To describe an act of listening is to describe not just the sounds you heard but to give a sense of how these sounds acted upon and within you, as a particular person in a particular place. Voegelin argues that listening itself is 'not only a physiological act but an aesthetic and perceptual attitude that influences how we understand the world, its reality, knowledge, and truth.' Maybe, when Margiad Evans declared that hearing was her only 'acute' sense, she was indicating that her acts of listening were the most important part of the perceptual attitude she produced through her writing. This idea is supported, in glimpses, throughout her autobiographical writing: 'led by sound up into the air and down below the level of the earth, consciousness roams while one's body rests.' Her mind only travels where sound has already been. Her consciousness becomes a kind of sonic effect. Elsewhere she describes the difference between brain and mind: the mind is 'always slightly *behind* in recording what is actually being done at the moment by the brain. It travels, like sound, behind the jet aeroplane.' The mind is compared to a sonic event, one of the loudest sonic events on Earth, and one that relies on a huge amount of resources and engineering – an interesting choice for someone whose most beloved sonic territory is the field, the garden, and the river. Inspiration, meanwhile, can be 'a torment', because 'the Muse' is 'a creature of midnight failures, who yet cannot be cut off, like a telephone or a wireless that is out of order, and *will* persist in communicating sound whatever one wishes.' Her writerly creativity was inseparable from her acoustic imagination, as her literary aesthetics were rooted in her physiological experience. Again, mental activity is imagined as a kind of machine, giving off a sound which she has no choice but to hear. If she ever had tinnitus, she would have recognised it as another sonic event which enforces listening, but she also would have found valuable new details within the relentless ringing.

Evans' writing frequently reveals new features of commonplace sounds. For example, in *Autobiography,* she discerns, in the sound of a waterfall: 'the overnote which has a scudding fleeting sting, like spray, and the thick spasmodic thud which is the body of water crashing into the pool.' She hears this sound while she's lying in bed. Her consciousness is led by her hearing, and her perceptual attitude teases out the details of a sound that's usually, in my experience, designated and diminished by one inadequate word, like roaring or crashing. The adjective 'spasmodic' brings out the muscularity of the 'thud', and the 'spray' given off by the falling water becomes the sibilant 'overnote', the hiss that seems to stay at the front of the sound as it reaches through the air to the ear. Evans' ability to dwell on sonic details, to describe sounds within sounds, makes her a valuable aid to people whose hearing is damaged. The waterfall description encourages me to update my descriptions of everyday sounds, to re-hear my surroundings through new words, making my auditory sensitivity a little bit more acute.

Autobiography is not in print – the last edition was published in the 1970s. I read it in the communal hush of a library. My tinnitus sounded loud against the faint drone of the air conditioning and the intermittent thumping of the exit doors. But that faint drone also carried a shudder, a rattle, and the softest of scrapes, and the exit doors, before they thumped, scattered soft footsteps from the carpeted corridor into the room, and those footsteps had varying amounts of thump and hiss that seemed to broadcast the mood of their owners for a second until the door closed, and the air-conditioning came back into focus until the door re-opened, and so on. Trying to describe my present sonic surroundings, as Evans might have done, encouraged me to project my auditory attention beyond my tinnitus, and re-discover that every sound is different, even two sounds covered by the same word, like 'footsteps', have endless variations, and that really, as Gertrude Stein once said, there is no such thing as repetition. If the hearing loss and tinnitus will always be with me, so will the constant interplay of other sounds, and while you don't have to be able to name something to notice it, the vocabularies employed by writers with acute hearing can help you to articulate the events that capture your auditory attention. Evans' textual phonography enhanced my sonic reality.

In Evans' fiction, most of which was written and published before her autobiographical writing, sound acts as a medium through which characters engage with each other and their environment. The critic Kirsti Bohata has noted how music 'is a recurring theme in Evans' depictions of same-sex attraction.' Miss Allensmore, the protagonist of the story 'A Modest Adornment', expresses her feelings for her partner, Miss Plant, 'through her oboe', playing 'an incomprehensible music' that 'sets her apart from the villagers'. Miss Plant doesn't play music, preferring to keep silent. But 'it wasn't a quiet silence: and it hadn't the length or loyalty needed for music. When Miss Allensmore played in her presence, Miss Plant would sit looking desultory, like a person who is taking part in a hopeless conversation.' In this story, Bohata notes that 'sound and silence are contrasted in place of, and sometimes as extensions of, lightness and darkness.' I would add that 'A Modest Adornment' also displays Evans' interest in audiographs. Miss Plant's peculiar silences combine with the noisy sonic belongings of Miss Allensmore, who as well as being a musician is 'an atrocious but, alas, perpetual cook.' In her kitchen there's always the sound of 'furious frying or the grumpy sound of some pudding in the pot, bouncing and grunting like a goblin locked in a cupboard.' These sounds combine anger and constraint with food, and suggest that Miss Allensmore, 'a fat black cauldron of a woman', swallows her emotions. The interesting thing about these culinary sounds is that Miss Allensmore always leaves her front door open. I think that the purpose of her 'atrocious' but 'perpetual' cooking must be to give her audiograph the widest possible audience. Her eccentric audibility maintains her presence in the village. Later in the story, Miss Allensmore is standing by her front gate.

> *She had a way of standing... with one hand just lifted as if to seize even a robin's twist of song, and catch it, as one squeezes a gnat. She was listening, anyone could see. She listened to every sound as if it were news. And she leant forward meanwhile in the attitude of one who is prepared to grab anything that comes close enough.*

Miss Allensmore here is trying to pluck sounds out of the air, to capture them, impossibly, and see how they feel between the fingers. By listening to 'every sound as if it were news', she aims to hear familiar things as if she hasn't heard them before, to hear her environment without relying on the habitual sonic descriptions that might dull her perception. She adopts a physical and mental attitude to hearing that doesn't privilege any particular sound – she'll 'grab anything that comes close enough' to be heard. The sad thing is that she doesn't want to let the sounds go, even though they will inevitably fade. Textual phonography might have helped Miss Allensmore. She might have found, through writing, a less acquisitive attitude to listening, and some acceptance of sound's ever-changing endlessness.

Wanting to understand more about my own sound-world led me into thickets of theory. As well as Voegelin's work, there was Alexander G Weheliye's *Phonographies: Grooves in Sonic Afro-modernity,* a massive project that brilliantly theorises the role of sound in black modernist culture through explorations of Ralph Ellison's *Invisible Man* and the work of WEB Du Bois. I had read *Invisible Man* years before, but on re-reading it after encountering Weheliye's writing, I was amazed by how much of its incredible sonic experiences I'd missed the first time round. Then there was Jennifer Lynn Stoever's *The Sonic Color Line,* which shows how, in America, 'white elites heard themselves as superior citizens, and they listened to themselves and Others through that privileged, circumscribed, and increasingly standardised filter.' And they still do, but they're not at all confined to just one country

One of the most physically disorientating – or

re-orientating – passages of sound theory I came across, however, was Casey O'Callaghan's notion that *sounds do not travel*. They stay put. They have locations. 'Sounds seem to come from sources in a sense that includes distance as well as direction, and not in a sense that includes travel,' says O'Callaghan in his book *Sounds: A Philosophical Theory*. We hear sounds because some events create sound waves, and it's the waves that travel through the air to reach us. The waves 'bear or transmit information about the sound events... and furnish the material for auditory experience.' But the sounds themselves stay right where they are. If you hear a sound moving, that's because its source is moving. I'd always *known* this, on one level, but I'd also never *admitted* it was true. For most of my life, some part of me imagined the sound and the sound wave were the same thing, and because the waves were travelling to me, I thought the sounds were somehow on top of me, covering or smothering my ears and bothering my body. When the distress of hearing loss and tinnitus was at its peak, I often felt overwhelmed, infuriated, and trapped by sound. These feelings were partly caused by my faulty idea of what sound is and what sounds are. O'Callaghan clarified my hearing in a way that helped my mental health. Suddenly, I could perceive all this distance between me and the sounds. There was a huge zone of auditory space beyond my ears.

Some Filters

Sound waves don't always stop at boundaries. The average wall will swallow the less powerful sound waves and reject the ones it cannot stomach. The more powerful waves, however, with their longer wavelengths and larger amplitudes, can stride through bricks and glide through glass. Most rooms' relationships with sound are leaky and promiscuous. Thumps and rumbles in other houses ramble into your head. To sound-proof a room to the highest degree, you need to build a room suspended within another room, to minimise the travel of vibrations between inner and outer. Or really, even better, you need to build a room-within-a-room within a room. That setup would be expensive. Another option, if you do not want to hear any sound from the rooms above and below and either side of yours, is to make sure that nobody lives where you live. That setup is also expensive, which is why we're all so used to hearing our bastard neighbours, whose unstoppable clunks and hoots we usually call 'noise', because we don't want to hear them, and the tension between their ongoing audibility and our wish not to hear them can be poisonous.

Most of the noises you hear in your home, if they come from outside your room, are the result of particular sonic effect: filtration. Your windows and walls and doors are filters that, as the urban planners and composers Jean-Francois Augoyard and Henry Torgue would say, produce a 'reinforcing or weakening of specific frequencies of a sound.' Filtration is when your walls swallow smaller sound waves and let bigger ones pass through. Spoken words might lose their intelligibility when they fall through a floor or rise through a ceiling, but the sounds that power them persist. Sounds heard through solid partitions, say Augoyard and Torgue, can provide the 'basis for shaping relations between individuals', which is a bit of an understatement if you've ever tried to live alongside a noisy neighbour. Filtered sounds can stab our emotions and steer our behaviour, and during low moments we might end up deliberately producing sounds intended to be overheard, so that the filters we share with other people vibrate with irritation.

When I lived in Leicester, I shared a house with a man who played the keyboard in a Beatles tribute act. He would often practise the song 'Lady Madonna', and its gormless melody would wander down the landing, round the corner, and through my bedroom door. The wood of the door and the fibres of the carpet would absorb the brightness of the keyboard's synthesised piano notes, leaving behind only the plonking lower-middle frequencies and the smug rhythm to trouble my trying-to-sleep ears. When he came to a difficult section the sound would cut out and loop back, which kept hold of my attention – a continuous sound would have been easier to ignore. I can't now think of that house in Leicester without hearing that song. The piano riff and its jarring interruptions, filtered through walls and floors and doors, stick to the memory, so that the memory itself is filtered through an unwanted, un-mutable soundtrack. Why didn't any of us ask him to use headphones when he practised? Probably because we knew that the sounds escaping our own doors and sinking into the carpets were no more appetising to him than his were to us. In the future, I would choose my housemates more carefully.

In Marcel Proust's novel *À la recherché du temps perdu*, Augoyard and Torgue find that 'we achieve a new step toward an understanding of the influence of filtration' on people. In a particular sonic incident, Proust's narrator taps on the wall of his room, and his grandmother, in the room next door, replies with her own distinctive taps:

> *Stamped with a calm authority, repeated twice over*
> *so that there should be no mistake, and saying to me*
> *plainly: 'Don't get agitated; I've heard you; I shall*
> *be with you in a minute!' and shortly afterwards*
> *my grandmother would appear. I would explain*
> *to her that I had been afraid she would not hear*
> *me, or might think that it was someone in the room*
> *beyond who was tapping; at which she would smile:*
> *'Mistake my poor pet's knocking for anyone else's?*
> *Why, Granny could tell it a mile away!'*

In this auditory episode, the narrator feels both a sense of 'contact' and a 'state of anxiety', an ambiguous filtered mix. The filtered sounds experienced amongst families are inevitably more emotionally complex than those heard between neighbours. The fiction of Deborah Kay Davies explores these audible complexities. Her writing contrasts the darkness of home life with the richness of nature; everyday cruelty and merciless humour come in equal amounts, and her sensory details always include finely crafted sounds. In her 2018 novel *Tirzah and the Prince of Crows,* filtered sounds carry serious emotional weight. The book's protagonist, Tirzah, grows up in the small Welsh town of Horeb in the 1970s. Her house is furnished with sobs and breaking furniture and the resonant silences of trouble. Her family are part of a religious fellowship who derive a strict moral code from the Bible that includes warnings like 'the flesh is the portal for sin'. Tirzah finds this dogma nonsensical, and struggles to live life on her own terms under the attentive eyes and ears of the fellowship.

Early on, when Tirzah is at her cousin Biddy's house and it's raining outside, we read about how filtration can shape emotions and memories. The rain 'throws itself at the sash windows, rattling the frames', which reminds Tirzah of the time when she stood in her own kitchen and witnessed her father, Gwillym [sic], destroying her garden before he 'concreted over the earth'.

Tirzah and her mother stood at the kitchen window
holding hands as he slashed the coloured heads
off all the flowers. Let this be a lesson to you
womenfolk, he yelled... banging the window with his
filthy knuckles. They could not hear him clearly, but
Tirzah recalls the look of his mouth and the sweat on
his forehead as he went on about women and their
fleshy, indulgent ways.

Here we have two filters – a present one and a remembered one – doing several different kinds of reinforcing and weakening. The first filter, rattled by the rain, calls up the memory of the second, banged by Gwillym's knuckles. Both 'rattle' and 'bang' describe a sound and an impact. Both filters reinforce the audible harshness of what's on the other side of them, and the less energetic rattle reinforces the memory, still active after two years, of the more energetic banging. What's weakened by the second filter is the linguistic content of Gwillym's yelling. Except for one sentence, Tirzah can only hear that he 'went on about women' as he tried, ridiculously, to reinforce the idea that the flesh is the portal for sin by destroying a garden. Her father produces, alongside his disapproving vocalisation, a spectacle of violence. Because her father is so vocal – so audible – in his disapproval of Tirzah's behaviour, Tirzah develops the habit of trying to assess the severity of Gwillym's moods by listening to the sounds he transmits through the filters of their house's walls, windows, and doors.

Later on in the novel, she is summoned to her father's study to explain herself after her parents discover she's been going to the forest to meet a boy. She first stands in the hallway and hears the clock in the front room making 'its usual uneven *tick-tock*'. She thinks of this sound as 'fighting – fast, then slow, fast, then slow – always the same,' alongside 'the faint noise of her mother washing the kitchen floor'. This brief interplay of filtered sound allows Tirzah to reflect on her position in the family. Through the filter of the front-room door, the sound of the clock, which is 'always the same,' provides an auditory metaphor for Tirzah's seemingly endless struggle against religious restriction as manifested by her father's moods. Certainly she is 'fighting', like the 'uneven' ticking of the clock, for her individuality and love of nature to be accepted against the rules of her father and her chapel. The struggling clock sound is set against the 'faint noise' of her mother, heard through the filter of the kitchen door, maintaining the house's high standard of physical cleanliness – a quiet auditory comment on what her family and community consider to be the lack of physical and moral hygiene Tirzah displayed when she met the boy. The sounds she listens to here, like the sounds Proust's narrator hears, maintain a kind of contact but without being entirely reassuring.

After this reflective interlude, Tirzah goes upstairs and waits outside Gwillym's study. She knocks on the door and calls him, 'quietly'. However,

> *from inside the room there is a silence so profound that it seems to press like deep water on her eardrums. Can I come in, Dada? She asks, tapping with her fingertips, pressing her straining ear to the door.... She waits a few seconds, then taps again. I'm going now, Dada, she says, her lips against the wood. Goodbye. Someone is moving in the room, but nothing else happens.*

The 'relation shaping' qualities that Augoyard and Torgue ascribe to filtration are present here, in that Tirzah's father is once again trying to assert his dominance through the production of unsettling sound. In this case, what passes through the filter of the door is an excess of silence, a slab of audible disapproval. It's interesting that Tirzah treats her filters with the same respect and sensuality she displays in her relationship with nature. She first taps the door 'with her fingertips', then presses her ear, and finally her lips, against the wood of the door. She searches the silence by physically probing the sonic filter through which it emerges. She's been told that the flesh is the 'portal for sin', and here she demonstrates that the flesh is also the portal for sound.

Fictional filters aren't only for difficult moments. As long as the people on the other side of the filter don't make you anxious, filtered sounds can be a source of pleasure. At the start of Marilynne Robinson's *Gilead,* the narrator, Ames, is writing a letter to his infant son, Robby, for Robby to read once he is grown up.

> *I can hear you talking with your mother, you*
> *asking, she answering. It's not the words I hear,*
> *just the sounds of your voices…. I never hear her*
> *sing except at night, from the next room, when she's*

coaxing you to sleep. And then I can't make out
what song it is she's singing. Her voice is very low.
It sounds beautiful to me, but she laughs when I say
that.

Ames listens as he writes, and he feels that what he hears is
important enough that he ought to record it in his letter. The
walls between the rooms filter sound so that Ames can't hear
any words, just the tones of voice of Robby and Lila, which
is enough for Ames to detect that Robby is 'asking' and his
mother is 'answering'. The exchange between Robby and
Lila prompts Ames to remember the times he's heard Lila
sing Robby to sleep. She sings a song Ames 'can't make out',
in a 'very low' voice. He only ever hears this event 'from the
next room'. This first instance of the filtration effect in *Gilead* shows how the acoustics of Ames' house contribute to
the meaningfulness of his life. As in the passage from Proust
quoted above, the sounds between rooms here 'maintain contact' between the family members. Unlike in Proust, however,
they produce no anxiety, but something more like a reverie.
The filtered sounds are also a way for Robinson to reveal Lila's
character by acoustic means. We can imagine Ames enjoying

these experiences of quiet listening in his home, in which his interior walls provide a contemplative acoustic space by filtering out those sonic tones that would make songs and words more comprehensible and thus less suggestive. All this filtration amplifies the distance between Ames, who is nearing the end of his life, and his young family. They communicate across their age gaps and the time-lag of the letter, as well as through the house's acoustic barriers. The subtext of impending separation is written, enacted, and sounded.

On a more superficial level, when Ames writes 'it's not the words I hear, just the sounds of your voices,' he inadvertently sums up what it's like to be amongst a group of people talking when you have hearing loss. I often think of this line in the pub. I can hear the people on either side of me, but most of the others seem to be moving their mouths and emitting tiny word-like sounds that never resolve into meaningful phrases. The people on either side of me can understand the sounds of the more distant speakers, and I copy my neighbours' reactions as if I've understood everything and it was indeed hilarious or awful or interesting. I could stare at these distant speakers' mouths and make a reasonable assumption about their topic of conversation, but I don't know these people that well, and I don't want to be a mouth-starer. I could ask everyone to speak up, but I don't want to draw that much attention to myself. The old question of hearing aids comes back. Why do I not have them? It's been years now since I had those hearing tests. I am comfortable and lazy. My consciousness is a room-within-a-room, and hearing loss has reinforced its immaterial walls.

There aren't really any sounds that are un-filtered. As Jennifer Lynn Stoever writes, 'a listening subject is comprised of auditory information processed through interactive and intersectional psychological filters that include the habits, assumptions, desires, and repulsions shaped by gender, class, national, regional, and linguistic identities.' Once sound has passed through the physical filters of walls or windows, entered the ears and reached the auditory cortex, it passes through mental filters shaped by social forces. Accents from the north-west of England sound like home to me, they are more comfortable, a better fit for my ears. Americans are exciting to listen to because they sound like films. My mental filter determines which sounds I find meaningful, which ones

I hold onto and which I let go, which ones are entertaining and which a threat. Stoever's book emphasises for me how human listening is filtered listening. Hearing loss has modified my ear's physical filter, but my sociocultural filter, with all its messy prejudice and daft priorities, is still in need of an update.

Filters can make us vulnerable to sonic intrusions. In May 1938, Samuel Beckett's neighbours bought a radio. The letter he wrote from his Paris apartment to his friend Tom McGreevy in London describes the radio like this: 'A terrible wireless has started next door. They turn it on when they get up, keep it on till they go out, & turn it on again when they come in. One morning it waked me at seven am. I must put up with it.' Beckett would live here, his first proper home in Paris, for the next eleven years. It's not clear how long he put up with the neighbours' radio, but I think however long it lasted, his experience of this unwanted filtered sound had a profound effect on his writing. It's absolutely characteristic of his style that he says 'I must put up with it.' Putting up with things is a central feature of his work. He could have written 'I must ask them to turn it down,' or 'I must get a wireless myself,' or 'I must find somewhere else to write.' But then he would have lost a reliable creative stimulus. The feeling expressed in 'I must put up with it' is the same feeling expressed by 'I can't go on, I'll go on' at the end of *The Unnamable,* and that appears in the first words of *Endgame* when Clov says 'Finished, it's finished, nearly finished, it must be nearly finished.' Most intriguingly, this feeling is still making itself felt in one of the last pieces Beckett produced, a short play for radio, known as 'Radio 1', published in 1976 in a magazine called *Stereo Headphones*. The two characters are 'He' and 'She' and near the start of their dialogue, She says, 'I have come to listen.'

> *SHE: Is it true the music goes on all the time?*
> *HE: Yes.*
> *SHE: Without cease?*
> *HE: Without cease.*
> *SHE: It's unthinkable! (Pause.) And the words too?*
> *All the time too?*
> *HE: All the time.*
> *SHE: Without cease?*
> *HE: Yes.*

> *SHE: It's unimaginable. (Pause.) So you are here all*
> *the time?*
> *HE: Without cease.*
> *(Pause.)*
> *SHE: How troubled you look!*

Here, nearing the end of his life, Beckett writes something intended for radio that dramatises the troublesome ceaselessness of the medium itself that he first acknowledged thirty-eight years previously. It is impossible to filter out everything we might like to filter out, from our minds as much as from our ears, and from our histories as much as from our houses. His neighbours' 'terrible wireless' did something to Beckett's filter – it made him pay attention to the temporal within the audible, how persistent sounds make us aware of duration, and how to listen to unwanted sound is partly to wait for its end. The absence of an end is 'unthinkable,' 'unimaginable', 'it must be nearly finished,' we think, after another day of enforced listening to someone else's Beatles practice, alongside our tinnitus, and alongside our suicidal urges ('the words too? All the time too?'). But the time always comes when things improve, when the neighbours go out, when the

'I can't go on' is over and the 'I'll go on' takes its place. Beckett's acts of exasperated sonic endurance provide reinforcement for my emotional filter, so I can more easily cope when unwanted words find a way through my walls.

One Sound in Particular

We went to hear the Aberdyfi Time and Tide Bell on a bright warm February weekday. The bell lives under a tall jetty. A small wooden staircase leads underneath the jetty to a platform about a foot above the water, where we sat down, half an hour before high tide, only a few feet away from the bell, which had been the object of an anticipation that stretched back a good few months. The bell, suspended by steel cables connected to the underside of the jetty above and the timber legs planted in the water, has an unusual shape: open at the top, narrow in the middle, and its lower section expands to a greater width than its upper one. It is the pale green colour of neglected copper or certain kinds of lichen. We hadn't realised we'd be able to get so close. It ought to start ringing as high tide approached, we thought. A vertical pole with a paddle on its lower end extended from the bell's interior into the water. The paddle moved as the water moved, moving the pole whose top end had a circular metal clapper that would strike the inside of the bell near its top. We watched this metal circle as it nodded close to the interior edge without making contact. We looked across the sunlit ruffles of the estuary and anticipated the bell sounding, any second now, within the glug and tap of the tide as it winced against the jetty's legs, and the hisses of our clothing as we shifted positions. Any second now, the bell would bong, we thought, maybe at first with a news-at-ten resonance and a faint crackle on the eardrum, and it would build in intensity and tempo as the tide rose, until it had the happy urgency of a jackpot. We watched the nodding clapper repeatedly not quite touch the bell's inside edge. Our attention hung around this highly visible silence and our anticipation rose and fell and rose again. We'd learned of the bell after the internet told us about the Zadar Sea Organ in Croatia, and a similar instrument in Blackpool, both of them built so that tidal water moving air through pipes produces an enchanting cloud of liquid hoots, and both of them too far away for a day trip. The Aberdyfi Time and Tide Bell is our most local tidal instrument, placed there by Marcus Vergette in 2010, one of several he has placed or intends to place around the UK coast. There's a legend that bells can sometimes sound from within the water around Aberdyfi, bells belonging to Cantre'r Gwaelod, the legendary kingdom said to have been drowned by rising sea levels thousands of years ago. Vergette's bell was going to sound out that story, any second now, we thought, and it would also toll for Tryweryn, the north Wales valley flooded in 1965 to make a reservoir to serve the people of Liverpool. Any minute now, the bell would lend its metallic voice to myth and history, its tones would ripple off the jetty's underside and the water's surface into our ears and through the water in our bodies, any minute now, with the leisure-screams of Outward-Bound kids jumping off the jetty's far end behind us, and our own voices compressed and slightly shimmering between the wooden ceiling and the liquid floor.

Twenty minutes of any-minute-now passed. A faint cramp came to the backs of my ears. We videoed the metal clapper's silent nod. We checked and re-checked the tide-times, squinted up the estuary for signs of surge or swell, cultivated our state of receptive tension or amused frustration, readied our brains and pores, our physical surfaces and our abstract planes, for the sonic event of the season, the aural confluence of public art and local mythology, metallurgy and politics, the audible and the tangible, the lost and the lucky.

Another twenty minutes passed. I tried to listen across the estuary to Ynyslas, to explore the furthest edges of my auditory attention. On the way to Aberdyfi, we'd stopped for a drink in Talybont, at a café run by the cyclist Gruffudd Lewis. Gruff told us his granddad once rode a horse from the sands of Ynyslas to the shores of Aberdyfi. Or was it that his granddad had known someone who'd claimed to have done that? My tinnitus whined. My tinnitus was time made audible. I could hear nothing else except the silence of the bell.

Helena sketched the view from the platform. I shifted position again. The bell sounded, an elongated thunk, a soft clang, the muted clink of the clapper surrounded by the bell-body's grainy hum, at the modest volume of a person saying 'well' or 'so'. We turned to face each other for the two or three seconds of the sound's dissipation, a single ring to mark the turn of the tide.

Bibliography

Jean-Francois Augoyard & Henry Torgue (eds), Andra Mc-Cartney & David Paquette (trans), *Sonic Experience: A Guide to Everyday Sounds* (McGill-Queen's University Press, 2005)

David M Baguley & Marc Fagelson, *Tinnitus: Clinical and Research Perspectives* (Plural Publishing, 2016)

Bella Bathurst, *Sound: Stories of Hearing Lost and Found* (Profile, 2017)

Samuel Beckett, *Endgame* (Faber and Faber, 1964)

Samuel Beckett, *Ends and Odds* (Faber and Faber, 1977)

Samuel Beckett, *Texts for Nothing* (John Calder, 1999)

Samuel Beckett, *The Beckett Trilogy* (Picador, 1979)

Samuel Beckett, *The Letters of Samuel Beckett Volume 1: 1929–1940* (Cambridge University Press, 2009)

Ella Berthoud & Susan Elderkin, *The Novel Cure: An A–Z of Literary Remedies* (Canongate, 2015)

Kirsti Bohata & Katie Gramich (eds), *Rediscovering Margiad Evans: Marginality, Gender and Illness* (University of Wales Press, 2013)

Elias Cannetti, *Earwitness,* Joachim Neugroschel (trans) (Andre Deutsch, 1979)

Brenda Chamberlain, *Tide-race* (Seren, 1987)

Deborah Kay Davies, *Tirzah and The Prince of Crows* (Oneworld, 2018)

Lewis Davies (ed), *Urban Welsh: New Short Fiction* (Parthian, 2005)

Margiad Evans, *Autobiography* (Arthur Baker, 1952)

Margiad Evans, *The Old and The Young* (Seren, 1998)

Margiad Evans, *Ray of Darkness* (John Calder, 1978)

Steven Roger Fischer, *A History of Reading* (Reaktion, 2019)

Niall Griffiths, *Grits* (Jonathan Cape, 2000)

Cynan Jones, *The Dig* (Granta, 2014)

Lewis Jones, *Cwmardy* (Lawrence and Wishart, 1978)

James Joyce, *Ulysses* (Penguin, 1986)

Brandon LaBelle, *Acoustic Territories* (continuum, 2010)

Ursula K Le Guin, *Words Are My Matter* (Small Beer Press, 2016)

Henry Miller, *Tropic of Capricorn* (Harper Perennial, 2005)

Casey O'Callaghan, *Sounds: A Philosophical Theory* (Oxford University Press, 2007)

Annie Proulx, *Heart Songs* (Scribner, 1995)

Marilynne Robinson, *Gilead* (Virago, 2005)

Bernice Rubens, *I Sent a Letter to My Love* (Parthian [Library of Wales], 2008)

R Murray Schafer, *Soundscape: Our Sonic Environment and the Tuning of The World* (Destiny Books, 1994)

Philipp Schweighauser, *The Noises of American Literature,*

1890–1980: Toward a History of Literary Acoustics (University Press of Florida, 2006)

Alan Sillitoe, *The German Numbers Woman* (Flamingo, 2000)

Richard Smyth, *A Sweet, Wild Note: What We Hear When the Birds Sing* (Elliott and Thompson, 2017)

Jennifer Lynn Stoever, *The Sonic Color Line: Race and the Cultural Politics of Listening* (New York University Press, 2016)

Lydia Unsworth, *The End of March* (Self-published, 2011)

Salomé Voegelin, *Sonic Possible Worlds: Hearing the Continuum of Sound* (Bloomsbury, 2014)

Alexander G Weheliye, *Phonographies: Grooves in Sonic Afro-modernity* (Duke University Press, 2005)

Ed Garland is studying for a PhD at Aberystwyth University, researching sonic experience in contemporary fiction. He works as a copywriter. He was born in Manchester, and lived in Leicester and Bristol before settling in Aberystwyth. He was recently longlisted in the Ivan Juritz Prize.

Acknowledgements and Thanks

I would like to thank the following people for conversations and comments that helped me to get this book written: Gwen Davies; Julia Forster; Matthew Jarvis; Gavin Goodwin; Cathryn Summerhayes; Elly Shepherd; Krishan Coupland; Catherine Donovan; Dawn Hart; Sean Wai Keung; Jim Pratt; Christine Sime; Michael Liggins; Clare Liggins.

Also, my fellow PhD students in Aberystwyth University's Department of English and Creative Writing: Eluned Gramich; Anna Beyer; Jennifer Dos Reis Dos Santos; Emma Butler-Way, and Sarah Reynolds.

And I would like to mega-thank Mary Garland, Peter Garland, Leon Garland and Helena Garland for providing me with life, encouragement, and mirth.

Praise for *Earwitness:*

A Search for Sonic Understanding in Stories

'Perceptive, beautiful... honest, truthful and succinct.'
Cathryn Summerhayes, Curtis Brown

'Intriguing, funny, learned, thoughtful and moving. Stresses
the vitality of literature to the development and sustenance of
the soul.'   **Niall Griffiths**

'A funny and occasionally poignant exploration of the sonic
dimensions of literature. Ed Garland deftly weaves reflections on
his own, self-inflicted, hearing loss and tinnitus with an analysis
of important but neglected textual representations of sound. This
book will change the way you listen to the written word.'
Professor Kirsti Bohata, Swansea University

'In this wise and searching book, Ed Garland creates a literary
sound map of Wales [and the world], an elegy to listening and
sounds he can no longer hear. Fascinating and moving. it makes
the (silent) reader perceive not just sound and the act of hearing
in new ways, it promotes "deep listening". Like all good art, it
alters our connection to and perception of the world.'
Kaite O'Reilly

New Welsh Writing Awards: Partners

The New Welsh Writing Awards were founded by New Welsh Review in 2015, to champion unpublished books under 30,000 words. Categories rotate, and to date have coverered writing on nature, travel, memoir, the novella, the dystopian novella, the essay collection and prose from Wales. This book grew out of Ed Garland's winning entry (originally called 'Fiction as a Hearing Aid') to the 2018 Awards, the Aberystwyth University Prize for an Essay Collection, **https://vimeo.com/271450997** (watch animated trailer for Earwitness). Warm thanks also go to our other longstanding partners: Gladstone's Library, Tŷ Newydd Writing Centre, Literature Wales and Curtis Brown. We share the mission of bringing great readers, writing and books together. Biblio-diversity rules!

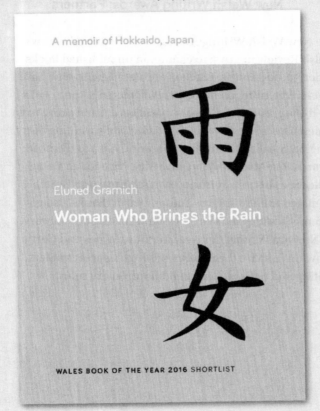

A memoir of Hokkaido, Japan

Eluned Gramich

Woman Who Brings the Rain

WALES BOOK OF THE YEAR 2016 SHORTLIST

'Quite beautiful. [The author encounters a culture that is completely alien] and she does it with a poet's eye... precisely and vitally. She reads this unfamiliarity with all her imaginative nerve-endings open: the effect is quite remarkable... [reminiscent of a] netsuke [in its] precision.'

WBOY shortlisting adjudication

'Mandy Sutter's Nigeria rises like a mirage [creating] a complete arc of innovative concision.'

New Welsh Review

BUSH MEAT

Mandy Sutter

'Triumphs, in its lean prose... humour... [and] evocation of a family divided by sexism and racism in 1960s Nigeria. Stitches together the threads of memory to create a moving tapestry of lost life, building bridges of understanding across time and place.'
Rory MacLean

Available from newwelshreview.com/rarebyte.php

NEW WELSH RAREBYTE

WINNER OF THE NEW WELSH WRITING AWARDS 2017

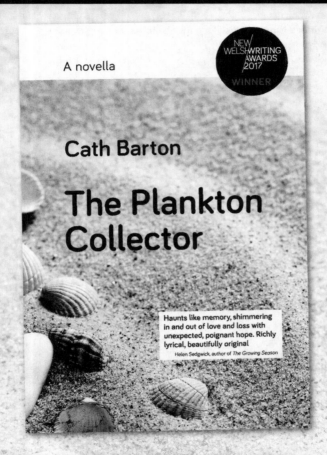

'Cath Barton writes her story... with such confidence and in prose that is so delightful to read, that I just couldn't put it down. It's beautiful. A delicate paean for coming together, full of understanding for the quirks and pitfalls and ultimate goodness in human nature.'

Mavis Cheek

Available from newwelshreview.com/rarebyte.php

WINNER OF THE NEW WELSH WRITING AWARDS 2017

'A powerful and moving exploration of the relationship of mind, soul and body... takes a topic often seen as a modern-world problem and reveals [it as] a far deeper issue, concerning one's relationship with the body in the physical world and the spiritual realm.... A moving insight into a trapped, questing state of mind and soul... a story of isolation and suffering, conveyed through beautiful and perceptive language... leaving us with a kind of shell-shocked admiration... and deep relief that she found her way to happiness.'

Frank Egerton, author of *The Lock and Invisible*

Available from newwelshreview.com/rarebyte.php

A memoir

NEW WELSH WRITING AWARDS 2017 WINNER

MY OXFORD

Catherine Haines

'This powerful, thought-provoking debut explores the author's experiences of her eating disorder in a narrative that is emotionally and intellectually complex yet unflinchingly accessible.'

Frank Egerton, author of *The Lock* and *Invisible*